Bloodline

Poems – Michael A. Griffith

THE
BLUE
NIB

Bloodline

Poems – Michael A. Griffith

Edited by: Shirley Bell

Cover art: Henrik Donnestad.   Design: Michael A. Griffith

ISBN 978-1-9999550-6-9

Dedications:
I can't adequately express how grateful I am to have my students, friends,
siblings, step-parents, Dad and Mom, Miranda,
and Sharon Ramos McClellan in my life.
You are all the stuff of dreams made real to me.
This book is for you all.
Sharon, you are my 1.

Contents

Polyglot

Sky-wide phoneme inventory
and obscure lexicons,

a cut of tongue
and cup of truth
to understand you fully.

To know true meanings and speak plain
as whales tell no lies in their arias
and bees are never false in their dance.

To whisper a word to the wind
and make the hurricane stop.

To speak to my elders as they sleep
and hum like a child as I drift off to join them.

To laugh in French and to sing in Welsh.

To read the Upanishads in Navajo
and to say "I love you" in Semaphore.

To understand me fully
cut to truth and cup my tongue
in obscure phonemes
and sky-wide lexicons.

Tetris

Refrigerator Tetris,
as I rush to pack your lunch.
The eggs displaced by the milk...
how old is that mango
and that Chinese take-out?

Coffee's just between
too-cool and cold,
but microwave re-heating
ruins any savory worth.

Cats are fed and off now to nap.
You're off to work as I prepare
to shape thoughts that
shape words that
shape
minds.

Mental Tetris
this gray January morning.
Time nobody's friend,
Time everybody's parent.

Naked

Braid lightning and thunder
like the hair of your stormy whore
or a virgin soon to be taken.

Call the storm your own,
usher in ruin and clouds,
rage when you feel forsaken.

Take us people, tear us asunder,
tell us you're making us great.
Build up your walls, your legacy of hate.

And rail and bully, throw the stone;
sling mud as you lie, even to yourself.
We will never be silenced, never be cowed.

You are accountable, we're keeping watch
as you display your tantrums and pouts.
Demagogue demigod, our naked emperor,
                                        proud.

beneath the rosebush

snake ribbon twist
round young sparrow
beneath the rosebush
full of thorn and bloom
shadows there amid petalfall
light there amid feathertore

garden tame garden wild
life cares for its own
snake don't care sparrow is scared
sparrow don't care snake is hungry
and there beneath the rosebush
rose just cares for rose

The Old Dinghy

Down along the shore
the old dinghy bumps the dock
forgotten by the son who once loved it.

My footfalls on his front porch,
my knocking on his front door;
sounds he'd come to resent.

The distance between us is not so great,
but the space...
it stretches out like darkness,

like the lake his dinghy is on.
Dark, even at noon, wide, can't see the other shore,
quiet and cold, this space between father and son.

Its paint's almost all chipped off,
wood gray underneath, sunbaked,
weathered as we have weathered.

Rust of time on our hearts like rust
from water on the dinghy's nails and rings
down along the shore.

Holes

Rudderless boat
Butcher, Baker, Prostitute, LLC
Should a storm wash them ashore
Deserted island,
At least they'll all have someone to eat.

The flies demand their lord,
Though a lady will do just as well
So long as her promi$e$
Ring true enough
And their multi-eyed glare she can meet.

The boat leaks
The three try to plug the holes
Try to keep it afloat
For this island Earth
Needs them powder-dry and smelling sweet.

The land they came from
Is the land of their fathers
And their mother Liberty is growing smaller
As they float off in their Sea of Words
And fill the holes until one will die in the heat,
One will die of deceit,
And one will rule over the flies.

Magazine Contents, July 2, 2017

Lazy Sunday editorial Trump, Trump, Trump

Tips for saving money as you travel
(I won't be traveling this summer.)

Five recipes using coffee as an ingredient
(I'd try three of them.)

A writer's memories of raising his daughter
(Nice and all, but my own memories are slightly
 more interesting to me, thank you.)

A poem with the word "bone" in it twice
(I've written a poem titled "Bone.")

Feature article: Our efforts to communicate with
 extraterrestrial life
(We can barely talk nicely to other countries or the
 man across the street. What, we hope E.T. will
 teach us how to be frickin' civil?)

What Ringo Starr has been up to lately
(Drumming and flashing the peace sign, right?)

Four cartoons, only one of which I really "get."
(I can draw better than *that*.)

Obituaries of noteworthy people
(Will I ever make that list?)

The horoscopes for the coming week
("Aquarius: July 5: Watch your back – somebody wants to
 stab it.")

Back cover ad for a resort with incredible white
   sand, glowing blue water, and palm trees
(and if I knew for sure the woman in the ad would
   be there, I damn well WOULD travel this
   summer, buddy.)

···and I wonder why my coffee went cold.

Textbook

Red heavy used textbook,
Contemporary American Poetry, Fourth Edition,
a reference and collection all-in-one.

I have owned it for some time now,
bought at some second-hand shop
or charity sale unremembered.

It is from 1985, from a year I could have owned
    it new.
I was a sophomore then; fresh, alert, attentive,
but this was never my textbook.

Now, this morning, I read through brief biographies:
Bishop, Brooks, O'Hara, Oliver,
then skim across pages of poems.

I stop at the picture of Galway Kinnell with
    a sloppy slim mustache dawn in,
then two pages stuck together by ketchup, gum,
    snot, or worse.

Across the poems of giants like Lowell, Plath, Roethke, and Sexton
are the tiny notes of a girl I could have known.
But she was never my friend.

I don't know her now, of course, though we'd be
    the same age.
I read "Her Kind" knowing that while other
    things feel more important,
for one semester at least, the thoughts of others
    were almost as interesting as her own.

The Professor is Still Talking

"Consider the difference
between the words *naked* and *nude,*
or *rock* and *stone,*"
the professor says.
"or, for that matter, *hug* and *embrace.*"

Pens and pencils move,
but not all of them writing.
Minds are moving, too;
not all of them considering.

My mind moves to you, naked *and* nude,
and then I remember the rock
                    (Or was it a stone?)
that cleaved my head when I was 10,

the solid crack of pain,
the blood in my eyes

A boy whose name I don't remember
threw that rock like a deadly Frisbee
and his teasing stopped
once he saw my blood.

All his stuttered apologies
lost within my mother's stony embrace.

My mind moves to you. I think of your hug,
as I think of you nude, not naked.
An ache, not a pain.

I embrace you after I hug you,
after I am made naked before you.

"*Embarrassed* or *ashamed*?"

The professor is still talking.

Satan's Toy Car

Let me tell you,
it was an August back before The War.
Mama and me sat on the front porch
watching the day pass us by like
a ol' wounded dog.

Hot day,
too hot to move much.
Flies buzzing 'round,
outhouse smelling real ripe.

Complaining did no good,
but we done it anyhow.

Day kept on limping by,
we kept on fanning ourselves,
sweating there, hoping
for a breeze what might never come.

What come was Satan.

Pulled up in a long red car.
A big city car.
Shiny, real shiny in the sun.
New.

He waves, comes up to the porch
carrying a black suitcase bigger'n me.
Smiles so big,
white, white teeth
mouth never touched chaw or a cigarette.

But he was still a bad, bad man.

Says he's got all kinds of stuff for sale
in that big black case. Jewelry, watches, toys, perfumes, soaps
   and notions.
(Not sure what "notions" are,
but the way he looked up at Mama
   when he said that word makes me think
they ain't good things for her or most any lady.)

Can he come on in and show her?

Well, he comes right up on the porch and
hands me a tin car he has in his pocket.
He says "Free. Just for you, sonny boy.
You take it and go play now."

Mama says my name like a angry pastor would
but I wasn't really going to take it,
'cause I knew Satan when I seen him.

That white suit, black shoes what never touched
   mud or seen dust on them.
Never been in grass.
His hair so oiled, forehead wetter'n my shirt was.
Too slick, too white, too clean in the damn heat.
Man just *had* to be Satan.

Kept trying to get Mama to
take him inside, to show her his stuff,
telling me to take the toy car,
red and shiny, just like his city car,
to go and play, he wants to talk with my mama.

He leaned in close to her
and she never stopped fanning her face,
   rocking in her chair.

He smiled real, real big
whispered so quiet I could never hear.

Then Mama, she stopped her fanning,
stopped her rocking,
looked Satan in his eyes
and slapped him so hard he went spinning.

Slap loud as a whip crack!
Satan's cheek red as his city car.
Him so angry he shouted every bad word on Earth,
calling my Mama names no lady ever ought to hear.

Yes sir, he go storming back to his big red car
thumping that big black case of his.
He threw that toy car off in the yard fast as
    lightning.

He drives away real loud and there's a big breeze.
Starts to cool off a minute later and a nice soft rain
    comes.
Makes Mama and me both smile and feel real good.

Day later I fetched Satan's toy car,
buried it up at the church
where it ain't done no harm
or no good ever since.

1

Logic counts in numbers
the heart cannot understand.
A math of mistakes and matches,
mayhem until numbers combine.

added, divided, subtracted, multiplied
(Don't forget to carry that "1.")

fractions,
          oh damn...
                    fractions.

Fractures of a family,
friendships add up to benefits
perks, peeks, pets
    (Sweat yet?)

                    Logic can go to Hell in its own tidy little
                              hand basket
          since the heart wants what the heart wants when the heart wants
                              what does her heart want?

                    (Why doesn't she call me?
              What, I'm not even worth a text?)

                    Okay: Breathe + breathe =

                    ...double-check the math...

              + (X-1) $\leqslant$3 $\div$ $\neq$ 1 ... = 2?

                    (Forgot to carry my one.)

Weave

Too many stories,
two too many faces to you,
Chimera with a lilt.

Fickle, thin-skinned,
yet tough enough to laugh and
to mean it.

Tough on those around you.
Rough around the edges.

I tell stories,
I show a face,
Minotaur with a maze to navigate.

Stubborn, thick-willed,
my laugh soon fades, but
I mean it.

Tough to let others in.
Rough to be near.

We talk
We joke
We laugh
We blush
We hint
We weave
a dance of words,   this dance of
intentions.

Our dance of glances

        not long held.

        If our eyes would stay, we would melt
            some of your roughness,
             some of my resolve.
            So we look away.

                You move off with shifting faces,

I go back into my twisting ways.

Growth

You run, run, Contrary, run from the garden.
Go!

Grow, grow, how did your garden grow?

No nasturtium, no nightshade;
passive posies and pale flaccid lilies, yes,
and the apple tree with its drooped fruit and
   blossoms.

You walk, walk over to the edge,
look back only once, for twice
and you'd never find the strength to leave.

Then you run, run Contrary,
run away, leave.
Leaves rustle and flutter by, leaf
leave now, by and bye.

Find your new spot,
plant your new garden.
Plant there among the bones and shale.

First year fallow crops,
ashy fruits, hollow hopes,
but weed out the bones,
work the shale to soil,
bleed, bleed life into that soil.
Work until you grow new life,
until you plant, root, grow
less contrary and
run no more.

Thunder on a Cloudless Berlin Morning

Papa gives me the capsule,
white and smooth, so like a candy.
He had it in a brass tube,
so like a bullet.

Mama is crying, her face in the handkerchief
Kurt and I gave her on her birthday.
It has violets and lambs on it.
I am her violet; baby Kurt is her lamb.

Papa goes and lifts Kurt from his playpen.
A soft kiss on my brother's blonde head,
then he sits Kurt on Mama's lap.
She looks up shaking her head, her eyes so wet.

Papa whispers to Mama, stroking her cheek,
"Shhh, now. It's the only way."
She won't stop crying,
won't stop shaking.

He stands suddenly straight, as if to hit her.
"Magda, look at our Elke. Look how brave! She
   doesn't cry.
She knows this is what our Führur wants."
Mama sucks a deep breath in and holds it.

Papa comes back to sit next to me, straightening his
   uniform jacket.
His medals are all polished, just as his boots and
   belt are.
So handsome, my doctor-soldier father!
He now strokes my cheek and smiles so brightly.

"You're a brave girl, my good girl, Elke."
I want to grow up and become his nurse.
I do well in school, but it has been closed for days.
Papa says the Russians and Americans are getting
    close now.

"Now," my officer father says, ordering his troops.
He takes up his capsule, whiter than his teeth.
Puts it firm into his mouth, but does not bite down,
and talks like the circus ventriloquist.

"Magda, *now*," Papa rumbles.
Mother groans as she takes her capsules from the
    handkerchief
and breaks one into Kurt's trusting pink lips.
He kicks his plump little legs, coughs.

She looks to Papa, then to me, then Mama shuts her
    eyes and bites her white, her white...

I can't look at her as she starts to jerk, and oh, little
    Kurt...

I look up at Papa.
His head is back, his mouth is open.
His mouth is white and open and he has spit-up on
    his uniform.

Kurt.
Mama.
My soldier father.

Sunlight through the drapes makes Papa's medals gleam.

I hear thunder coming close now and the sunlight is
   so bright.

I look down at my hands in my lap
and see that I have crushed my white capsule.

Bloodline

Line of blood spills out like syrup
a split instant following the surgeon's scalpel
just under my wife's swollen belly.

She lies there in dozen-hour labor stupor,
arms stretched out on the operating room's crucifix table.
Small inverted Christmas tree angel of a woman,
saintly, delirious, and prayerful.

I don't look down at her face;
the blood and what follows hold my eyes wide
   open.

Our daughter is lifted from the wet cavity cut across
   my wife.

No blood on her;
it is all on her mother.

Sound swirls around us,
many voices in a loud hurry to be heard:
numbers and words thick with terminology.

My daughter, in given statistics,
a weight and a rating,
by these loud fast people.

A procedure to them,
a miracle to me.

Widow's Walk

The cliff.

       The rocks and waves below.

Off the widow's walk you, widow, still walk

at dawn, near noon, at Venus's first showing,

in heat, in chill, in rain,

       rain,

         rain,   ripping-wind
                      rain

  Your children know not where you go

     know not any hidden intent,

       so long as they're fed, cooed and
                     hummed to.

The call.

That blackest sea.

Look, look again, look out on horizon bright.
Ships pass, none, none with your husband's flag.
Look, look still, down to those waves, those
                     rocks.

Hear a call?

Cliff's call for you to leap?

It mocks!

     Water's cold call, drown down as your husband has.

      Your children call, turn to fetch them, hold them down, drown.

They call.

   Papa...

     ...he is...

home?

Brenda's Truck

Back behind the shed
the old Chevy rests
where it's rested more years
than Brenda's dad's been dead.

Bed's all rusted-out,
dry-rot's claimed the tires,
and weeds grow up around the body
of the once-rumbling blue truck.

The body's still good,
and you can't kill a truck's engine
unless you really try.

Men have stopped by quoting prices,
making offers, each different every time;
higher in the fall, lower in springtime.

The money, the men would be of help, she knows.
But neither come by in winter, so why bother?

Besides, Brenda sees dandelion-yellow butterflies
land on the truck every summer and she knows
her dad's spirit comes with them.

And she knows she could start that truck up
any time she set her mind to it.

Glass Woman's House

The glass woman,
seen whole only in reflections of others,

there in her glass house of shrinking windows
   and growing shoulds,
a stone's throw away from being revealed.

Shines in her sorrows,
shimmers in her fears,
shakes in her solitude.

Throw that stone, boy,
hurl the brick,
but aim away from the glass woman.

Hit her sorrows and fears,
strike the solitude and break
those panes of should;
take up a mallet and ruin her house of oughts
   and wishes.

Let her shimmer in the light shining
from strength she never knew she had.
Then help her build a new house that's not so
   fragile.

Gem Show

Tanzanite. Dinosaurs dancing as emojis try to talk
Charity popcorn in five flavors. Autism speaking
as several cancers spread.

Aquamarine. I care about cancer more now that
        we are in love,
but I still don't fear my death.

Amber. Fly with me. Be still with me. Get stuck
        in me

Diamond. Shine just for me. Dance only for me,
Talk to me.

Jade. Be old with me.

In Weatherly, Pennsylvania
(For Sandy Drusda)

Her trees will not last the year, she knows,
the man from licenses and safety for the city
   came by
and left a letter telling her to cut them down.

Tall as any she has ever seen,
these trees have seen more than five generations
    of weather,
winter, and warmth. Infestations and storms
    couldn't hurt them

until the last bad ice, heavier than lead.
Tall but deformed now, defaced by this unkind year,
her trees try for austerity, try for the clouds, try

for strength in April's chilly winds,
as she tries to catch them with her sketchpad.
Her trees will not last much longer, she knows.

Ash

To leave us the way she wanted, she held
her tongue, hid the diagnosis until
her illness would no longer be denied. It stripped
her power over the truth as it drank
her strength and ate her resolve.

No longer denied, the cancer became
a glutton for attention simply by being
there. Her weakness, her pains, her clenched lungs,
our tears; near-constant callers and over-staying
    guests.

No to therapies, no to drugs stronger than
Advil p.m., no even to in-home aides until
that last week. If the dying can't be
selfish in dying, when can they be?

No to a funeral, no to a viewing, just
spread her out around her yard
and her garden; let the wind and the rain,
the sparrows and squirrels carry her off.
If life can't take away the dead,
what is worth taking?

The last coughing, the wish for
one last smoke, sweet as
that first one, and 26 minutes later
our tears visited again.

The cut man

The cut man bleeding out
time in his bathtub ballet
astride one good foot, hands
on slippery walls as the other foot
crumbles
to mud.

Water runs, water washes,
showers down   time   an impure thing
runs a ring around him.

Twin terrorists Age and Infirmity strike as one,
some graceless balance,
a trigonometry uniquely his own,
cut man, the mud-foot man.

His balance always off,
his dance of elephant steps.
Water runs as time runs away
dirty.

Run no more, cut man,
clay man.
Time to stitch time.
Time to dry mud to cement.

Listening to Johnny Cash

Listening to Johnny Cash with my friend Arthur
    in his room at the nursing home...

I can only understand about every third word
    that Arthur says, but it's alright,

Johnny says enough for any three men.

Shut

In the nursing home hallway she sits, eyes
shut too tight to really be asleep;
tall with a slim grace almost gone.

There is so much astir around her, and
she doesn't decrease it any,
even as she sits soundless,
those sleepless eyes shut so tight.

What nightmare lives in
that tornado alley mind
that could scare her so
and keep her awake,
shut her apart
from me?

Even if I asked, she couldn't tell.

So the world moves and passes. Aides
speak to her, but her answers
are nonsense whispers
as her lips go slack.

And when she finally does open those eyes they
    shine. They shine
like a sky cold enough
to form frost, vast enough
to lose a man, turbulent enough
to blow away any nightmare.

Noona

You called me "honey" amid your clutterspeak.

You will forget what you said to me
or that we spoke once you turn and leave.
You will roam the halls,
look into darkened rooms
for someone only you might see.

You will moan and wail and cry.
Wet will drip from your nose.
And the next time I see you, you could be calm.
You might even be laughing,
yet your eyes never seem to dry.

Only remembering patches of a life before,
thoughts so full of holes,
like the ivory doily
on your cluttered night stand,
brought here with your family pictures and more.

In your walker's basket is all that matters:
Crumbled tissues, your stuffed toy, a bag of
   crackers,
an old church bulletin,
a younger woman's rosary.
Jumbled things, memories in tatters.

Nursing home now your forever place.
Few here know your story;
none of us can tell it fully.
And you can't share it with us;
you only remember a trace.

Words hold so little meaning now.
Use them still, some real, most not.
You understand you, we try to distract you.
Redirect, try to get a smile, to calm you,
give you some peace, but we don't know how.

We call you "Noona," though you have no
grandchildren to seek.

Esther

(For Mary Handl)

And she will come again,
but this time will be the last.

This woman of many coats,
but only one good outfit.

Slowing down, slowing,
she feels it
but is not quick to admit it.

And as she comes again
she brings gifts to be treasured
long after she has gone.

Acknowledgments:

Sincere gratitude is given to the following sources for first publishing the poems listed below, some in different form:

Art Villa's Poetic Life and Times: Holes

Creative Talents Unleashed: Thunder on a Cloudless
   Berlin Morning

Degenerate Literature: 1

Dissident Voices: Naked

Door is a Jar: Ash

Night Garden Review: Shut, Widow's Walk

Persian Sugar in English Tea: A Bilingual Anthology of Short Poems and Haikus (Volume 1): Esther

PPP Ezine: Growth

Ripen the Page: Noona

Scarlet Leaf Review: Bloodline, Glass Woman's
   House

The Blue Nib: beneath the rosebush; Gem Show; In Weatherly, Pennsylvania; Listening to Johnny Cash; Magazine Contents, July 2, 2017; Polyglot, Satan's Toy Car (as "The Day Mama Slapped Satan"); Tetris; Textbook; The Old Dinghy; The Professor is Still Talking;

www.ingramcontent.com/pod-product-compliance
Lightning Source LLC
Chambersburg PA
CBHW071228170626
46809CB00005BA/1979